T0032346

LUCKY WRECK

ADA LIMÓN

LUCKY WRECK

15TH ANNIVERSARY EDITION

POEMS

AUTUMN
HOUSE PRESS
PITTSBURGH, PA

LUCKY WRECK
An Autumn House Book

All rights reserved.
Copyright © 2021 by Ada Limón
Typeset in Minion Pro
Cover design by Kinsley Stocum
Cover art by Stacia Brady
Printed in the USA
No part of this book can be reproduced in any form whatsoever
without written permission from the publisher, except in the case
of brief quotations embodied in critical reviews or essays.
For information about permission to reprint, contact Autumn House Press,
5530 Penn Avenue, Pittsburgh, PA 15206.

ISBN: 978-1-938769-80-1
LCCN: 2020948839

All Autumn House books are printed on acid-free paper and meet the
international standards of permanent books intended for purchase by libraries.

"Autumn House Press" and "Autumn House" are registered trademarks owned by
Autumn House Press, a nonprofit corporation whose mission is the publication and
promotion of poetry and other fine literature.

Autumn House Press receives state arts funding
support through a grant from the Pennsylvania
Council on the Arts, a state agency funded by the
Commonwealth of Pennsylvania, and the
National Endowment for the Arts, a federal agency.

www.autumnhouse.org

CONTENTS

INTRODUCTION

The most terrifying thing about writing the introduction to your own first book, fifteen years after it was first released, is closely reading your own first book. I expected to meet a stranger, someone naive and very different than what I remember, but *Lucky Wreck* is not a stranger at all. *Lucky Wreck* is me at the beginning, at a doorway. It is, quite simply, where "I" began.

I wrote this book while I was processing my stepmother's terminal illness, the chaos of my own ethereal relationships, and the overwhelming presence of mortality that was so oppressive after the towers fell in New York City. Despite the recognition of death, there is a resilience here that surprised me. Now, nearly twenty years after some of these poems were written, I feel almost envious of that resilience. I need some of that now.

Since this book was released, I have led so many lives. My stepmother has been gone ten years now, and my days, my life, look both softer and harder from how they looked then. I am no wiser, but I have experienced so much more. Audre Lorde once wrote, "Our feelings are our most genuine paths to knowledge." I have always maintained this is true for me as a poet. I trust feelings more than wisdom.

Today, these poems feel like a much-needed interrogation of life. An interrogation I'm still doing daily. Language has always saved me. The way we can play with it, surrender to it, lose ourselves in it. Wreck and recover on its shores. Even now as we enter the deep throes of the pandemic and a great grief lands on the shoulders of the world, I continue to find comfort in poetry, in language, in the recognition of beauty and longing and survival. It is a strange human endeavor to write it all down, but I am so grateful to have made this book that first ushered me into a life of words. I am so thankful for those that helped me along the way.

Someone asked me once if *Lucky Wreck* was how I'd describe myself. And even after all this time, I suppose it is.

ONE

First Lunch with Relative Stranger Mister You

We solved the problem of the wind
                          with an orange.

Now we've got the problem
                          of the orange.

Jimmy once said, *Do you get along with everyone
                          as good as this?*

I did not know how to say yes.

In Albuquerque yes is hard/easy/look
                          a roadrunner!

You there, across the table, could be my opposite
of enemy. I do not want 8 babies.

Are you hooked on height?

I'm trying to stop myself from telling you
about the time I lost my passport

and so thought of killing myself,
identity being an important instrument
of my behavior.

I saved myself by thinking I'd write a novel
and then fell asleep in the closet.

It's called, the novel, *Last Things for Lala.*

It is not called, *The Contradictory Nature of Hangers.*

What is the punctum?

Out of which limb will you grow?

Jimmy had two sons, nice ones.
Two taller than me. I bought them food and listened
to ICP in the 65 Chevy.

I was 53 years old. That's one year older than Jimmy.

I've never been where you live,
but that doesn't mean I should move there.

I get attached to rocks.

At the tone the time will be: *Let's never die!*

We've just met, should we move to Ensenada?

Or should I just borrow a pen?

I could tie your shoelaces

                  together and play king

of the mountain.

I've brought a lot to the table.

You've brought an orange.

I'd rather sit a kiss than you would.

My fist is like a kiss.

I want a shirt that says, Kiss Me or I'll Cut You.

I want to start every sentence with,

                  Let me tell you something, Mister.

Mister who smells like yellow.

Mister who has too many pockets.
Mister who is a Mister times two,

Mister who misses and then gets sad,

Mister whose lunch I'm having.

What to do with the problem of the orange?

Let me tell you something Mister,

you've got to peel it.

Little Day

This is what it comes down to:
Me on a park bench, always writing,
This is what it comes down to.

The Great Erector of Invisible Pets

Let me start again,

> it didn't take place in the meadow,
> and I wasn't pretty.

Having lost a bet about a minor thing—dog fights or cockfights,
these recent hallucinations— hard to tell,

I found myself outside the weigh station,
picking paint chips off the wall.

Someone had stolen my shoes.

In the distance, the man at the end of the field became an elk grazing.

I had an important question, it came in four parts:

1.   Where are my shoes?
2.   What's so bad about eating lead?
3.   Could it be a vitamin deficiency? Can people be unleaded?
4.   And then there is aluminum?

There was a strange intimacy of pavement and heat, offensive!

No one answered.

The grainy lead chips looked like bleached bones.
I arranged them in order, like vertebrae,

and I didn't want to touch it when it was done, I wanted to
build a flesh house for it, and let it crawl.

I wanted to stand over it and wait
> and when it was tired, I would let it rest,
when it was hungry I would feed it.

When it had questions, God damn it, I would give it some answers.

This Darkness

This darkness is not the scary one,
it's the one before the sun comes up,
the one you can still breathe in.

A Little Distantly, As One Should

1

I keep wanting to write about
accidents and how I hate them and it's so
obvious. Everyone hates accidents.

So, instead I've been watching
my neighbors set up their picnic table
and tent (do you call it a cabana?).
The man is wearing a bandana
and a leather vest without a shirt, a look
I've never learned to appreciate,
even though I am from California.
The woman looks like that bartender Kim,
but younger. I've overheard that they're
expecting company in approximately 45 minutes.
I have noted the time. I'm excited for them.

It's hard to be excited for things,
not the same way as I used to, or maybe
it's just that I don't get stoned anymore.
Jake and I listened to a Neil Young album
in my old apartment over and over
again for hours. Every time I tell someone that he's
died, that same image pops into my head.
He's sitting on the windowsill with the light
behind him so you can't see his face.
I'm very aware that he's younger than me.
He wasn't stoned. Jake was a good kid.

My friend, all the time, says *I'm so excited*,
and when I ask her, for what, she just shrugs
and says, *Aren't you?* I suppose so. Yes.

2

Up on a mountain near Lake Tahoe,
I once fell in love with a boy named
Billy, or was it Bobby? I was thirteen
and he was humoring me. I needed humoring.
We had driven to the campground
in a huge blue station wagon my dad
had rented on account of our gear.
It felt unsafe. Station wagons for all their air
of safety always feel unsafe to me.
The way nuclear family should sound
comforting and yet it only ever sounds
like something that's going to explode.

If you've ever driven to Lake Tahoe
you know the roads. Long curving
gray snakes of pavement edged by
mountains and those drop-offs. I hated
them, still do. But when you have to
get somewhere you drive on them.
(I have to tell myself this all the time.)
You can't really stop going places
because you're frightened.

It's like that road sign that's the image
of rocks falling down a mountain
on to the road. I never knew what you were
supposed to do about that, duck?
Is it saying that inevitably a rock will
fall on you? Is this good that we know this?

I am obviously unsure of the usefulness
of inevitable things. Even the word
inevitable is awkward and hard to spell.

I never kissed Bobby or anything,
although I probably should have.

3

Sometimes I think the memory of an event
is better than the event itself. The way
the retelling of something is satisfying.
That's why it's so unsettling when I can't
remember everything in detail.

I want to remember the exact song
that my brother and I were singing
in the back seat of that rented station wagon.
All that I keep thinking of is "Respect"
by Aretha Franklin. I can't imagine
that's what we were singing, but maybe
that's why it stands out. It was unusual,
like the car and the roads.
I can convince myself of anything.

My neighbors (the my there is so endearing,
it makes me love them) have finished
with their cabana and the Kim lady is power washing
the chairs. They are laughing and getting
along well. She doesn't mind his vest.

Now, I am almost positive it was "Respect."
Seeing them in print can help the facts become fact.

When I think about it, I would like to go back
to Lake Tahoe when it's warm out and swim.
That's where Jake was when he died.
The car went off one of those roads
I mentioned earlier. (I was going to tell you then,
but it was strange to write it down.)

But now, the guests have arrived! (They were
21 minutes late.) The vest is lighting
the barbecue and one woman is pregnant
and in overalls. The whole thing is so domestic
and soft you can almost wear it.

4

I have gone out to the fire escape
and come back now to my desk. I wanted
to be there with the neighbors for a while.
The Kim lady waved and I waved back,
a little distantly, as one should, as if
I cared only a little, as if they were only a fleeting
thought and me, simply a body on a windowsill
passing through.

Little Morning

I want to be the doctor of your mind
tying your shoes, laying you to rest.

I want to be the doctor of churches,
the kinds of churches that have picnics.

I want to be the doctor of telephones
and I'd walk through the black wires.

I want to be the doctor of mattresses
and pillows, and comforters and nights!

The Echo Sounder

"*echo sounder* n. A device for measuring depth of water by sending pressure
waves down from the surface and recording the time until the echo returns
from the bottom." —*American Heritage Dictionary*

1

She enters the world a ready-set-go girl.
She comes with a list of things she cannot
see, she comes with a language restricted
by its own inability to name things
as she sees them. She believes that there are two
worlds and she lives in the one that is
separate from the other, the seed that comes
up outside the garden, the one door with no
handle, the shingle in the roof with the
weathervane, the arrow flying from the quiver,
the child who can balance on her palms
and is hated for it. She wears no shirt,
still no one speaks to her. She speaks to
everyone. She has a bicycle and a family,
but it does not matter. She is difficult to
catch, she knows all the names of all the
fish, she is aware of them dying all the time,
upstream, the sockeye and the coho,
upstream, the Chinook and the king,
upstream, to the sand and rock nest of their
deaths. She thinks the bodies decay too quickly.

2

When she is eleven years old, she thinks
her body will be like that of a fish. She does
not want to decay before she uses it.
She is confused in the dark. She is never

scared. She is convinced that she can talk
to God and she asks him a question.
She does not get an answer, so
she makes one up. She believes the answer is:
everything stops, the food is in the mouth,
but the mouth is not there,
the water flows, but there is no creek.
She understands now that bodies can swing
from trees and whole families can be
locked up, that people die the way fish do
starving sometimes, gutted and tortured
by children who think they are being
scientific and responsible. She thinks God
must know this and therefore he is ugly.
She decides God is no good, but he must exist,
he must exist so she can hold him accountable.
She decides this and then forgets.

3

At one point she decides she is in love,
the way she woke one day and thought
she had dreamt up the word *Philadelphia*,
that there was no other word in the world
as beautiful as *Philadelphia* and how
she planned to make it mean something,
like the way everything can
touch you at once, the mason on the billboard,
the old theater's neon sign,
the water towers next to the cross,
the curve in the road where the school bus
stopped, the wet smell of boots and dirt,
the feeling when all those things get to you

and you want to cry or pray and because
you're no good at either, you
tell everyone to leave you alone so you
can go on feeling the world climbing around
in your body like you were just as much
a part of it as it was of you, maybe, she thought,
she could call that feeling *Philadelphia*.
She fell in love the same way.

4

One week she thinks about offering,
how it is difficult to offer something of yourself.
She thinks it should be easy, how she
has an echo chamber in her chest. What
she sends out should reflect and return.
She goes to the creek on one
trip home and sits there for longer
than she planned. She decides to estimate
how long she will live and then she says
this is when she will die. She says it again,
This is when I will die, as if the repetition
will endow the words with nonsense, the way
a word becomes no longer a word, but a strange
sound that animals make, she takes comfort
in her animal-ness. She wants to go on
being an animal, not something that represents
something else, but the original object, the
thing before it is named, the fish before she
knew it was a fish, when it was just another
lost thing, individual and shadowy, working
its way toward its own end.

The Different Distance

There is little I can say about this distance
except that it is something I do not own.
My distance is pinker and sleeps on the floor
next to the breathing sheets. My distance is not a distance
at all but a closeness so close to close it's closer
to fear than flying.

Selecting Things for Vagueness

I want to know some things
for certain, and other things
for vague. Have some vague idea
of where you are, not an address,
no train stop, no telephone,
no relative, no neighbor, no local,
no highway blah blah blah, no turnpike,
no regional, no county, no watershed,
no school district, no supermarket,
no tributary, no mailbox, no corner,
no state bird, no "as the crow flies,"
'cause what I'd do when I find you,
well mister, this I know for certain.

The Way Things Have Been Going Lately

I've been thinking of moving someplace
warm, buying a pick-up, and keeping the radio
turned to the highest level. Everyone thinks that
now and again, right? I hope they do it. My friend,
Ms. Red did it. (She lives in New Orleans now
with two turtles and some boy I've never met.
She signs every letter on the outside with the date
and the temperature. The letter I got today
said, *May 11th, 88 degrees in the shade*.)

There's a restaurant in my hometown called
The Ranch House, serves Mexican food.
It's right off the highway and if you sit in
the window you can read all the large billboards
welcoming people into town. The food's
pretty awful and it's dirty, but for some reason
I want to go there right now. I want to be welcomed.

Sometimes I think I am angrier than
most people, but when I think of this river
up in the Northwest that I once walked
and swam in for miles, I think I could be
so full of light that it would be hard
to hold me back from missing even where
I am right now, but how do you hold
a river in your head before it turns
straighter and black, unfolds into asphalt,
into some mean road rolled out before you.

The Worth of a Thing That Is Not a Thing But a Number

All the houses are burning
                    like you do

with the ache of newspapers
                    stuffed into

the wood and behind the bricks. 1908. 1926.

News.
News.

I prefer to think no one lived here
                              before me.

I sing like this: *I am the only one, I am the only one, see.*

My dream: my social security number is a ton
                              of tiny zeros.
But it's not worth much, worth
                    less than a phone number.

Gilbert from *Anne of Green Gables*, the movie,
is entirely responsible for why I say *sorry*
                    like a Canadian.

I also think Canadians shake their heads funny when they clap.

Take the point off a needle and a finger
                    and you've got some kind of safety

that provides only reruns and parking lots and reruns of parking lots.

I used to live there. I was quite happy.

I got engaged
by the automatic window-ness of it all,
and to air conditioning too.

Air! AIR!

And everyone is a full-grown child.

My number?

My dream: I give you my social security card; it flies off like a hawk moth
                            lands on one of those houses on fire, the ones I don't live in
                            anymore, at least I don't think I do.

Gilbert was a good man.
He shook his head when he clapped,
                            like a real Canadian.

In the pavement place, I was good at cooking, and good looking,
                                          and at counting. 18.21.52.

            Now I'm not that good at any of those.

But Gilbert did say, *Being smart was better than being pretty.*

Little Kindness

My kindness is wrapped around my ankles
and it is too heavy to fit in this door,
too ugly to wear out.

Farmers' Almanac

According to the *Farmers' Almanac* the best day to slaughter animals
is the 25th of this month. And all my horoscope said today was,
                              Hooray for the differently sane!

The country I occupy is different than yours, but we both pretended
the vegetable steamer was a spaceship at one point or another
              and watched it real-fly to the kitchen.

My brother once pounded nails into the wood garden fence in the shape
of a hot rod. And then drove a hot rod in it. It was a hot rod inside a hot rod
              and I fell in love with men forever.

You there, I am collapsing, is it as
adorable as it feels?

Sincerity is what my meal is made out of.
              July 1st will be the best day to eat a meal of sincerity.

At the dinner table I still sit on my knees, like I'm praying,
              all the time, for more trouble.

One thousand toothpicks represent one thousand soldiers
              in the child's history report.

One thousand toothpicks represent only one thousand toothpicks
              in this report

but they still cannot stop gravity
from burying the things it tugs.

According to the *Farmers' Almanac*, this month, I am one more than falling
down,
I am down falling,
I am catch-less.

To manage to miss things is an improbable act, to refer to people
as things proves that I miss more of myself than others.

According to the *Farmers' Almanac* the master of invisibility finds
himself dining, too often, alone.

In my country exploding things come from the inside like a sparkler
and everyone notices and wants to warm

their hands on your burning body.

If I meet you again, let's make inappropriate sounds
all over town and by inappropriate I mean the sounds
                                   of our names.

Little Obsession

I am not obsessing.
I am just sitting here
perforating this Post-it
with a pushpin.

The Lost Glove

does not miss the flesh of your left palm,
instead it is content in its bed of grass and
garbage. You, also, do not miss the glove.

You watched it go. On the way to the bar
you passed it. Old Red found it once,
brought it in. You looked away

into the bottled mirror, which was not
away at all, but rather, back at
you, all the while it pointed, the rips in the seams

opening like one thousand mouths. No,
it does not want you back. It wants people to
know who sits on the bar stool is a liar,

an absentee landlord, and how you forgot,
how the goldfish forgets she's already eaten
and goes on drinking her air. You felt the

fingerprint of something, but not the finger,
almost a pleasant pressure, walking backwards
through a door, until, the leather wet with April,

the inside rotted out like a body, it found its way
to the curb and became all things dismissed,
the anger blistering in the throat, the handcuff

of obligation and it lay there, in the daylight
saying, *Do not forget what I accuse you of*, saying,
do not forget that You are the you in this poem.

TWO

The Circus Folk Find Fault in Their Own Humanness

The circus of us
            is constantly leaving,
the elephants down the midway,
my little bone baby, my tented
world of un-machines.

Yes, we've killed most everything:
the Caspian tiger,
the Javan
and, it's true,
the Bali are all gone.

Still, our finest failure,
            our human parts uncovered and
            raw like a tiger wound
we cannot find a reason to touch one another
without a gasping audience in the room.

Miles Per Hour

The painted tiles are riddled with blue
cornflowers and unnaturally green stems,
as unnatural as trying to concentrate
on the blossoms covering the bathroom walls,
the way when we were driving 66 miles per hour,
and each lupine had become not one,
but rather one massive stain of purple and blue,
like one large bruise covering the right side
of Highway Twelve and the more I tried
to find one leaf, one petal, the more dizzy
I became until the search for something
simple had ruined its way into nausea, into
that throbbing in the middle of my eyes
when we knew it was over, all of it and yet
we were still in the car, still going to meet
the family and when we pulled over on
Old Sonoma Road under the tree to make
love once more before the parental hand
shake made love more difficult, more
permanent, my head swelled not knowing
whether or not to hold onto the handle
or the stick shift or to shove my foot
on the dashboard or just to remain pinned
like that, pummeled in the car seat, what we called
screwing, the hard stuff, the times when we were more
angry than anything else, the turn-on being the
pain. And through the car window I could
see everything in summer heat, the oak leaves
the tires had crushed in their masculine heaviness,
the fungus that grew on the side of the tree making
a shape like a face or a birthmark and each single
thing made me grab you harder, want to be connected
to something larger, as if we could swell into the

universe itself, the movement of hips propelling
us up into some, I don't want to say celestial, body,
but something as big as that, where we could watch
over everything, the towns growing smaller like
little painted toys, those giant oaks and cedars,
turning into a brushstroke of blue and green, small and
unrecognizable as these flowers now, painted
haphazardly and scattered, like the memory
itself, the car driving farther and farther down
the highway, my face pressed up against the window
unable to discern whether or not I was as much
of a blur as the things I passed.

The Firemen Are Dancing

I am running my finger through the rough knotted hole
on the edge of the stained, oak, bar table.

It looks like it could be an eyehole and I think it
would be the scariest thing in the world if I were an ant,

a hole where the bottom drops out, just like that, on to the floor.

I don't want to drink tonight, or if I do, I want to drink a lot, enough
to lie down on the ash blackened floor and watch everything
through the eyehole.

Everyone is talking about parties, the vice cop keeps looking
at the guy we call Red and that's fine by me
because I don't like him, never have.

O and the firemen are dancing. My favorite part is how
they are dancing so close.

One is pulling the other to his hip and one with the hat is laughing
and tossing his head back as if they were seventeen or, even,
as if they were alone.

And it's okay that I don't have a specific *you* right now and it's okay
that I'm not sure who this *you* I am speaking to is anymore.

The firemen are dancing and one of them has leaned his head on the other's
blue shoulder and the ones at the window are singing
and watching with big, lovely, fireman smiles.

And it's okay that you weren't here to see it, I'm going to tell you
all about it. Even if you never ask, I will.

Little Monogamy

This is done at a particular angle.
This is done level, done plumb.

I am no longer a public space.
I am worldwide to one.

The Unbearable

My grandmother only wants to tell me who died
and how. She tells me of all the traffic accidents
as if she was reading a menu to me out loud.
The man who was decapitated while driving a
tractor trying to make space for a new
Stop and Shop. The woman whose eyelashes
started growing inward until it was so painful
all she could do was lie there and scream and
then finally, not scream anymore. Over the kitchen
table I told her to stop it. She didn't
understand why it was making me upset.
It's what happens, and as she was trying to explain,
in my mind, I had already left the room and walked
up the street to the house I grew up in and laid
down outside on the green cement. In the shade
the cement was cool and hard. My old cat,
Smoke, came up and sat on my chest,
the way she never would when she was
alive, and in the trees there was a woodpecker and
squirrel bustling on their branches seeming very alien
and small. I have a friend who says, that sometimes
when she thinks about animals, she starts
to cry and right now even my dog is dying,
yesterday when someone was petting him,
he collapsed as if the weight of the hand was too much,
as if being touched, even in love, was unbearable.

Spring, 1989

—for Carmina

1

Acacia thick in the air like horsehair,
flies in the yellow mustard weed, flies in the mind,
and the spring of Ramón Salcido returns
like remembering a film in a foreign language—
images in a dark room, a nodding without you.

To be in a small town, is to repeat the same
experiences again every day, as if each day
of seventh grade, the same girl told me what
finger-banging was, and I drew a picture
of a spider on my silver binder.

And then Ramón Salcido entered, an automatic
villain, come from the vineyards,
come from the river border, from Agua Caliente.
The rumors, like the three-pronged poison oak, a murder,
another murder, his three girls found with their throats slit
in the county dump.

2

Some say the valley is a perfect climate
for growing the most delicate of fruit, the varietals.
We prided ourselves on our madrone trees,
the smell of oak all the way up the switchback
of Trinity Mountain, and down into Tortilla Flats.

The night of the murders, they put Becky Lambert
on Channel 2 news, to interview her about
the climate of fear, locking of doors,
and everyone else was terribly jealous—
she looked pale and perfectly concerned.

In Diamond A Ranch, where their estates
were listed in the paper, as updated and upgraded
and the only things of color were the dark-eyed
junco and the western scrub jay, in the fields of
Sobre Vista, people were worried.

3

In a small town, reports come in waves,
one large game of telephone and talk back,
and soon facts were confirmed, a dead wife,
two dead girls, six counts of manslaughter
and the third daughter found still alive,
her throat slit.

Say something and you'll be better
than most of us who walked into our classrooms
and bent toward the afternoon continuum—
the horse flies more interesting than most days,
their slow lumbering thick in our uneasy room-air.

I would like to say it brought us closer
together. O bless the shared tragedy. Disaster
on the mainland! But the truth is no part
of a story, or rather not a part that anyone believes;
one girl lived, and they found Ramón Salcido
in Mexico six days later and now he believes
he's found God.

But to be in a small town is to repeat the same
experiences again every day. Sixteen years later,
the same bright reflection of traffic underneath
the new yellow of spring heat, the cars going both
up the mountain, and down, everyone looking over
their shoulder for a dark enemy and one girl,
over and over, returning to us—in a familiar shape,
a good object, a hope in the weeds.

The Angles Made at the Factory

Try to remember the angles of devotion
that happiness is undone by, like the blue-belled
dress on the factory floor. She left it there,
even though she was so cold after the machines
stopped churning the air. She stood naked
in sawdust behind a stack of sheet metal
waiting for him to find her girl-dress, make
a move toward her girl-ness. Come behind the metal,
come behind the metal in sheets. The angle she stood
to watch him stoop over the blue-belled dress, the angle
he stooped over the blue bells; these were not right angles
mind you. He did not see her there, her feet tiptoeing in pine
dust, but he came nonetheless on her girl-dress
and her angles learned to grow some kind of sharpness.

The Ladybugs Grow Bolder Every Year

Disappeared I was, or was longing to be so,
when all the options showed up exhausted

and arrogant in their soiled woolens and ash
stains from the bar. I had, once again, taken

refuge under the coffee table. My body against
the brittle floor, laying pain against pain, a good

match. And here they come again, trying to save
my life; the ladybugs of this town are insufferable.

Still, they seem like good little horses, bearing some
resemblance to "things which belong outside"

and none of them with a barrel of brandy or
a bible, yet I imagine myself into that one red thing.

How pleasant to be no longer human, no heart
in the brain, no scolding for lying on the floor,

but also sad too, how these clear wings hidden in the hull
reminds the living body of where it cannot go.

All Kinds of Shipwrecks

The television is playing a show on shipwrecks,
and this voice is my favorite voice:

the voice that tells you where the treasure's hidden.
The structure of us is not a structure at all,

sleeping sideways on the foldout couch like visitors.
"We are not permanent here," the steel springs say,

and then the TV again, that sound so underwater smooth,
and how is it that they always find the wreck?

It is seven in the morning, another boat, another treasure.
Now, I am watching TV upside down, and what would I rather be:

the diver, or O lucky wreck to have been found?

THREE

The Spider Web

1

The orb spider continues to spin a whole
Road map of a world on our large
Black living room window,
Each thread a highway to its charge.
The intricate lace of white lines stuck
Where a fly waits for his nip and his tuck.
It is so sturdy it will hardly ripple,
The house has to shake for it to shake even a little.
As the cars pass, it is solid as it is strobed.
Headlight after headlight, the same high beams
Run like upside down waves on the ceiling.
But the web holds the fly anxious for the final blow.
I watch as the spider comes close like a spy,
Unsure if I am jealous of the web or the fly.

2

Unsure if I am jealous of the web or the fly,
Both of them sure of their beginnings and ends.
I slip into bed and lie there beside
Your body like a buoy that the ocean resents.
If I could just grab hold and find a way to paddle,
If you could stop dragging your feet along the gravel.
As a child I remember knowing how to float
When sober was the wind and my body, the boat.
Now each step is anchored and you continue to drift
In the room where we pretend that we are alive,
Where you and I commit the sin, and you and I forgive.
This is not holy but I wish the winds would shift,
Let some higher being take back the power,
As we mistreat our bodies, minute by minute, hour by hour.

3

As we mistreat our bodies, minute by minute, hour by hour,
Day by day, the laundry piles up like driftwood and debris.
There is no coffee in the kitchen and the milk's gone sour.
I won't dust the living room so the spiders are free
To march in the corners and over piles of mail,
Like prisoners who've recently overthrown the jail.
Open a window, I can hear a voice in my head,
Get dressed. Get out. Wash the sheets on the bed.
It's not God, I tell you. It's my mother,
Though there is little difference between the two.
I'm convinced that together they're planning a coup.
She'll say I've got two problems, I'm one and you're the other.
She's right you know the tide is too high.
But we could drown in a glass of water, you and I.

4

But we could drown in a glass of water, you and I,
Lying in this knee-deep pool of self-pity
With no intention of getting out or getting dry.
You argue that there is a freedom, a simplicity
In dropping beneath the usual swing of things.
But I am the one who keeps listening
When you start to speak as the television fades
And you begin your wallowing on the downside of day.
We must have some belief in this small life,
I still throw salt over my shoulder; you play the lottery.
There are nights when we make an effort to agree
And drift into bed where our bodies collide.
What would happen if we answered a letter or the phone?
Are we scared to discover that in fact, we are not alone?

5

Are we scared to discover that in fact, we are not alone?
That the windows open out and the wind blows in
That there is something familiar in this unknown
Need to protect our minds, our bodies, our skin,
And each other. You make me floss every night,
And worry now and then when I lose my appetite.
I want to lie down on your inconsistent shore,
Make myself a sandcastle and draw myself a door.
Come on, come out, or simply let me be
Alone and watch the waves pull their fingers back.
Instead, you hold me under until my body goes slack
In this living room sand by this suburban sea.
I've got no compass, no lifeboat, no mast, sail or stern,
Only the small prayer that, tomorrow, the tide will turn.

6

Only the small prayer that, tomorrow, the tide will turn
And the net will come up full of feast has the hope
To break the silence in this house and make us unlearn
Our habits, our tracks or untie the knot in our rope.
Can a spider change his mind and cut the noose?
Can a fly lift her wings and pry herself loose?
Let's test the waters, drop the anchor, watch it sink
Into the waves the way you drop yourself in drink.
I will not enforce a curfew or try to hide your vice,
I may be blinded but I'm convinced we can stop,
Slow down, get right or simply watch the boat rock.
I will be the empty vessel and my heart the ice.
Pour something in me, the time is wasting.
I am the one doing the spinning and you, the tasting.

7

I am the one doing the spinning and you, the tasting.
Your spinnerets spread your silk like a staysail-stay,
From my vantage point I can see the land erasing
Off the horizon and the night becoming day.
I'm not fighting anymore, tied to your mast
I am watching the web and the shadows it casts.
If I had my choice, I'd have a boat of my own,
The sails would be my skin, the bow my bones.
I'd paint a spider on the side and make it my omen,
Like a remembrance, a tattoo, of the life I left behind
You could stay in this room with loathing on your mind,
I'd fly the flag and name her, *Unmanned Woman.*
Still, I remain, trying to weave self-control
Where the orb spider continues to spin a hole.

FOUR

The Lessing Table

The dinner table was too small
and that was obvious.
We had to buy smaller forks,
smaller chairs, stop talking.

You took the saltshakers
off. I decided I'd only make
soft foods so we wouldn't have
to use knives anymore.

It kept on shrinking for days,
the butter taking over the dinner
plates, the green beans looking
longer and mean,

until it was just a thin slip
passed between us, a note
on blue-lined binder paper
in number two pencil:

Make the train wheels lock.
Make the mobile stop.
Do something, do something.

Little Flower Funeral

How well you do! How good you are!
Little flower, little dirt eater, little time passer.
And when you die, little flower, how lovely
the time will be then; we'll all take turns
twisting your body around our fingers and our
opposable thumbs. We'll put you in our hair, little flower,
because you've died for us and that's nice of you, and
truthfully we'll understand you better then.
We'll tell stories of your bravery at longevity around
the campfire and how you grew even when you
swore you wouldn't go on. Little flower, we'll
love you more when you die, don't hate us
for not telling you sooner.

Centerfold

Crouched in the corner of the barn,
we sat with the cedar chest splayed,
and the magazines laid out in perfect
piles. I was the first to reach the
centerfold and together we stared.
These women, these giantesses,
folded over couches, on bear rugs,
or steel bars, their bodies so slick
they could slip through the pages
and then through your fingers.
One, in particular, was my favorite,
with her left leg perched on a ballet bar and her
hair piled around her shoulders,
I thought she must be famous.
I thought how lovely it would be to
be her, to be naked all the time,
and dancing.

Little Commitment

Is it bad to want to commit
because one is so tired?
The child so overwhelmed
that when the bell rings she stays in
from recess, just to be very quiet
and draw a clown on her desk.

Evolution

Come quick to the breaking.
Gather on the thick tar
rooftops to see the kid
jump, or not jump,
just wait. Bottle caps
and beetles are embedded
in the sticky black of
summer. O, the uselessness!
There was a large tree
once, big enough to hold
all of us and we each
had our own tree house.
We shared things,
molasses, crackerjacks,
cigarettes, and we had sex
all the time and it was fun.
Who was it that decided
to come down? Was it you?

The Frontier of Never Leaving

If the wound you cover is made of sheet metal
and iron gates left over from the junkyard
of Forever Worried, and the school of Always Broken,
here, I have saved you a seat. If you have hidden your
outlawed books in your mattress and your outlawed
thoughts in your hands, here, I will give you refuge.
This is what I heard underneath it all, underneath and in the
beginning but now let's move to Canada. I hear it's nice and
they don't kill each other as often. I can even forgive them for speaking
French. Really, not all of them speak French. But would I miss it?
If I move to Canada and there's no war in the Spring,
I won't miss Iowa, that's for certain, but it's the only thing.
The fields keep growing longer like a veil between us,
the mountains like sutures on the map, and yet they are
ours, the way mustard can be ours off the highway
and windmills in the deserts and roads, even roads. Barbed
wire between us, fences between us. The roadrunner has
run into the river and Misters, you do not care. Another puzzle
piece of my American map has unfolded. I am the only
thing that fits together here, in this frontier of Never Leaving.
Today, I am going to play the record of the revolution
everybody is going to sing along and the more we turn it up,
the less the flag will wave over you and the more it will
become a swallowtail and migrate to our houses, the little ones
in the back, the ones with the lights in the window. Look!
You can see them now, opening their doors in the fog.

The Different Ways of Going

I keep calling that bird in the window a *flight risk*
while watching you get dressed from the bed.

And it's remarkable how a mood can change everything,
like a car accident.

Your footsteps have a color, if you could call it that,
                          the color of wool uniforms.

This weather makes me wonder how many hands I've held.

I'll never see you again, but that's a note I tear up in my mind.

Two days from now I'll be in a field, picking peaches
and feeding the retired police horses, with names like Bullet, and Justice.

On the field, we call it the long one, I will come close
to a hawk in the oaks, I will say, *That bird looks like a flight risk*
and no one will hear me except the hawk and the blue into which it goes.

13285 Arnold Drive

Shadows black my moon-white legs where,
          in the back seat of the car, I lie facing upwards in my favorite game,
eyes to oak tree branches, to telephone wires.

Now we're on Dunbar Road, now Arnold Drive, Warm Springs.

My finger runs down the seam of the gray seat cover,
          streetlights strobe the window and my parents drive in silence,
or in something like silence. They do not hear me navigating,

Now we're on Henno Road, now we've passed the bridge.

All this I tell by the trees, the black turns of road and highway,
          until we've passed the pink lights of Shones Market and
our gravel driveway groans beneath our wheels.

The first time I found you in the darkness it was like this.

Your body outlined like a map within a map,
          moths once stuck in screen doors fluttered by the porch light.

Now I am at your belly, your armpit, collarbone.

Outside the acacia burst into yellow flares of pollen
          and rubbed against the windows, its skin the color of cement,
its branches loaded down with directions and

I don't understand how each unit of pollen flies so far, lifts on pockets of air
          and travels, like a spaceship, or a rocket,

or how each one is self-sufficient in its yellowness,
          traveling north of south or just straight up,

living life in spasms of movement, over rocks, whole towns, cities,
          and never being able to name things,
to own them or to not own them, to find a way or to lose it.

Thirteen Feral Cats

1

Forgive me, I have broken
more than most of my own rules.

Let me lay this (I'm pointing to my body) on the table, simply,
and you can lie under the table and we can stare at each other.

When people in your life get sick, everything changes like a color.

I have refused to remain silent and yet
still remain
very small.

I have made out with you in the restroom.

I'm sorry I was playing *Name the Things in My Room*
while you were speaking:

> 1. An old painting of a woman and a tiger.
> 2. A desk full of damaging material.

(What is a deciding factor? How can I get one?)

Now is this a touching game?

Now is this a running game?

In my primarily winged soul, I have
managed to misconstrue this wicked racket and have fallen again.

Honestly, I don't want to kill anything right now.

Thirteen feral cats in my backyard, I don't feed them;
                              they live off garbage and luck.

2

After returning from the hospital, I inquired
about fixing the feral cat colony issue:

Thirteen feral cats, I said, *Will they be euthanized
or do they have a chance for adoption?*

I said, *I worry about them,*
I said, *I dream about them,*
I said, *Will they be okay?*

To round up a colony of cats I would have to trap them myself. One cat a
day, 13 days, 13 cats. A cat trap: $250 deposit, a rental fee: $10 a day.

And then what? Do you kill them?

I have recently taken the elevator with a bee I found stuck in my office.
                    I carried him in my hands down 6 floors to the lobby
                    to let him outside.

I said, *Don't die bee*. I said, *Go to the park bee.*

3

Ah the art of making our strange disasters suddenly public.

Thank you for joining me
            here in the middle of this oxygen tank.

I have made out with you in my hallway,
                    by the mail slot.

But what's left of celebration,
            the brass band of confidence and perhaps, beauty?

Does my hand fit necessarily in this door jamb?

    If so I will hold the door open for you.

And can we wander? Can we sit a while on this bench?
What world grows this shadow?

I have set out like a ship among ships,
but do not hold my own escape against me,
    it's too cold.

4

I am not a captain nor a patient,
    still I am steered by illness.

And the women do come and go, and the men too and the men too.

Through the kitchen window, I can see the quiet conversation,
    the one that Fall brings and lays upon
    the table like a pheasant.

The mad keeper of numbers is always present,
the mad keeper of numbers is making a noise like

    the slow hum of traffic passing, the people
    in their cars watching us on the median—pointing
    at this shock of stillness.

5

The man in the khakis asks an unnatural question,
it makes me think of the word *khaki*, its awkward, ugly
world of military and republican.

If I could wear a coat to stave off stupidity and redundancy
          I would not call it alcohol or friend.

In the hospital it is not good to be sober, nor is it good

          to be caught stealing, but worse
to be caught feeling
          better than anyone else—
          your beautiful body reeling

around the room like a windmill
          above the blue beds of tubes and metal.

Tell me again the one about the doctor who used the word
palliative. I bet he wore khakis.

Is it this window that opens?

Outside there is a persimmon tree—the unpopular fruit—
the color of destruction.

The tree is dying, black bark coming
up from the wintered ground
                    but still, its fruit, those tiny
offerings of sour and pucker,

                    those last colors on earth,
keep growing out
of anger at the dumb god that made them
so persistent in life.

Who tells a tree to stop
                    growing?
The highway to become a dead end?

I have come to believe that faith might be a room
with four walls that you can visit from time to time—

the walls made of steady light one can pass through or
                                        not see at all.

If you're lucky, you can return there
even afterwards—and it will still look the same,

not like the room I have seen, the walls covered

in moss and mold,
the floorboards breaking on reentry,
the door often locked.

6

What does it mean to be your own New World?

I can barely stand
               alone in the shower sometimes.

It's mornings most that I miss
               the holding of hands.

I want many hands, hands that have come and gone,
hands that no longer exist except in cutting short a lifeline.

I would like to say I just want one hand—to name it my own.

But it's so dark in this doorway and so full of infinity.

7

Once a cloud, with whom I lived, drove by the prison
          he had been caged in.

          We could only get so close.
          But of course, he was not a cloud at all, you know that,
          he was a man, almost sorry for the walls
                              that held him for so many years.

He seemed to think the walls were unbelieving
in the thing which they had been asked to do.

To become a cage in the desert.

But nonetheless we threw bottles from the car window
and he became a cloud again, floating above
          the road, dangerous
to those who wished to see.

How we wish some things to be undone—and only ever lose our buttons.

But still there are days where I want everyone to come home—
          the largest dinner bell in the state of longing.

The original sense of rapture, the being overcome,
overwhelmed by a presence.

Driving through Arizona and his thoughts of these unbelieving walls—

I thought, how the human body is asked to
cage things as large as the ocean,
          fantastic and moving but also
those dark things too.

8

In case you were worried, the cats are doing quite well.

I've named each of them.

9

Sometime last night, I heard the shuffling
of cards in a man's laughter.

> I have a deep belief in the shuffling of cards—
> the necessity of re-ordering.

He was playing the guitar and the room felt like a fire feels.

I thought of her in Stanwood, the real her, the one whose poem this is,
> not the men or the friends, or the you's, but she who has been
dealt the raw hand of horse dung and cluster flies.

The idea of sickness is not so much an idea anymore.

And I was not thinking of her blood cells or the flip charts,
> I was thinking, *She'd really like this song.*

10

If everyone in the office agrees, collectively,
not to talk about the moon,
could we "not-talk" it out of the sky?

Make a blue hole in the night.

Someone might suggest hanging
something up there:

an orange, a pomegranate.

But the moon cannot
       be replaced by a bruisable thing.

And I'm told, some spaces cannot be filled
but only altered or cut away.

As in the story I heard about a captain, returning
to his ship after too much drink.

As a prank, his mates had replaced
       his compass with a heart-shaped clock.

All night, in his bunk, he turned it up and down, but always
he was in charge of his direction.

Those stubborn hands were unmoved by his anger
and finally, on the deck, in his stupor, he found the moon.

I'm told, this captain, with his heart in his hand,
was, for the first time, truly amazed as he found north
to be in the heavens

and all at once his small life made perfect sense.

11

The Buddhists say, *It is of our nature to die.*

But that doesn't seem enough, does it?

The bees in our body released—the wasps in the heart.

Once, above where a woman nursed,
       a wasp nest grew in the ceiling.

At first only a tiny discoloration,
the spreading stain of larva pupate
only looked like an upside down puddle.

No one wanted to kill them.

The child in this woman's arms only
one month old, the wasps growing along with him.

We wanted them to grow up and leave eventually,
                                        the wasps and the child.

But what grows in us and around us may
                not always be protected
                by mandates of good nature.

One wasp nest contains 3,000–5,000 wasps.
Nineteen stings is considered the lethal dose
        of wasp venom for a full-grown adult.

When the first leg dropped through the plaster and paint,
white dust landed on the child's forehead.

By the sixth leg, everyone was out of the house,
                until soon all the wasps were dead,
                white poison covering their
                small bodies still preserved in their home,
like a tiny, winged Pompeii.

12

One must mourn things daily
as a cause for continuing.

So, all the wasps died and I saved one bee.

But they were each real. You could touch them.

Outside the cats have made a bed out of an old blue tarp
the neighbors used for a boat.

I am hoping they will grow impossibly old.

Not forever, just as long as the moon.

> Say tomorrow I come to a stoplight
> and pass a man I knew once or twice.

By now, I have shortened his name
to his profession, *the baker, pharmacist, butcher.*

Let's say there's little between us, except the obvious street.

What remains is a cold kindness
> the way a supermarket clerk says,
> *Thank you for coming,*
> but doesn't really mean it.

But then there is also something else.

It happens quietly, not often, but on certain clearer nights,
two boats coming up over the waves:

> *Look*, we say, our arms waving at one another,
> *We're alive, look at our dumb luck!*

13

This morning when I opened the screen door,
the cats were standing on a wooden ladder next to the house,
                    one for each rung,

at first glance they were after nothing, scrambling for oblivion,

until I saw the bee, lazing its circles above them near the roof.

When the door slammed, they turned as if to say,
                    This is why we've come here, for this moment,
                    to chase anything that might get away.

As if we were put here to remember our own ending,
                    to wander out into the streets,
                    (their own brutal oblivion)

to stare at the tree's dark bark, to know that in order to go on,

                    we must accept the cage we are given
                    that someday we will be released,

                    into the unimaginable

and until then, praise the walls
                    and all the parts of us they manage to hold so dearly.

ACKNOWLEDGMENTS

Grateful acknowledgment is made to the editors of the following journals where these poems, sometimes in earlier versions, first appeared:

Another Chicago Magazine, Winner of The Chicago Literary Award: "Miles Per Hour," previously titled "The Highway"

Brooklyn Review: "Centerfold"

Cubby Missalette #13: "Evolution"

Cubby Missalette #18: "Little Day" & "Little Obsession"

Gulf Coast: "13285 Arnold Drive"

Iowa Review: "The Lessing Table"

Poetry Daily: "The Lessing Table"

Slate Magazine: "The Lost Glove"

Spoon River Poetry Review, Editor's Prize Finalist: "The Echo Sounder"

Tarpaulin Sky: "The Frontier of Never Leaving"

Watchword: "All Kinds of Shipwrecks"

My unending gratitude to my remarkable family: Stacia Brady & Brady T. Brady, Ken, Cynthia, Cyrus, Emily & Bryce Limón.

I am greatly indebted to those who have read and edited these poems in their multiple forms over multiple years: Brady T. Brady, Stacia Brady, Jennifer L. Knox, Trish Harnetiaux, Heather Grossmann, Jason Schneiderman, Joel Israel, Salvatore Scibona, Shafer Hall, Barry Witham, Jimmy Santiago Baca, Phil Levine, Marie Howe, and Sharon Olds.

I also owe much to these fine institutions: the Provincetown Fine Arts Work Center, New York Foundation for the Arts, The Community Word Project, LaHaye Art Center, Readers' Books, and the Turkey's Nest.

And lastly, thank you to the dear departed Jean Valentine, who chose this book 15 years ago and launched my uncertain boat onto the sea.

ABOUT THE AUTHOR

Ada Limón is the author of five books of poetry including *The Carrying* which won the National Book Critics Circle Award. Her fourth book, *Bright Dead Things*, was named a finalist for the National Book Award, the Kingsley Tufts Poetry Award, and the National Book Critics Circle Award. She's originally from Sonoma, California and lives in Lexington, Kentucky.

Photo credit: Lucas Marquardt

New & Forthcoming Releases

No One Leaves the World Unhurt by John Foy ♦ Winner of the 2020 Donald Justice Prize, selected by J. Allyn Rosser

Lucky Wreck: 15th Anniversary Edition by Ada Limón

In the Antarctic Circle by Dennis James Sweeney ♦ Winner of the 2020 Autumn House Rising Writer Prize, selected by Yona Harvey

Creep Love by Michael Walsh

The Dream Women Called by Lori Wilson

"American" Home by Sean Cho A. ♦ Winner of the 2020 Autumn House Chapbook Prize, selected by Danusha Laméris

Under the Broom Tree by Natalie Homer

Molly by Kevin Honold ♦ Winner of the 2020 Autumn House Fiction Prize, selected by Dan Chaon

The Animal Indoors by Carly Inghram ♦ Winner of the 2020 CAAPP Book Prize, selected by Terrance Hayes

speculation, n. by Shayla Lawz ♦ Winner of the 2020 Autumn House Poetry Prize, selected by Ilya Kaminsky

All Who Belong May Enter by Nicholas Ward ♦ Winner of the 2020 Autumn House Nonfiction Prize, selected by Jaquira Díaz

To view our full catalog, please visit <u>autumnhouse.org</u>